C000145144

THE
AQUARIUS
ORACLE

THE
AQUARIUS
ORACLE

INSTANT ANSWERS FROM
YOUR COSMIC SELF

STELLA FONTAINE

greenfinch

Introduction

Welcome to your zodiac oracle, carefully crafted especially for you Aquarius, and brimming with the wisdom of the universe.

Is there a tricky-to-answer question niggling at you and you need an answer?

Whenever you're unsure whether to say 'yes' or 'no', whether to go back or to carry on, whether to trust or to turn away, make some time for a personal session with your very own oracle. Drawing on your astrological profile, your zodiac oracle will guide you in understanding, interpreting and answering those burning questions that life throws your way. Discovering your true path will become an enlightening journey of self-actualization.

Humans have long cast their eyes heavenwards to seek answers from the universe. For millennia the sun, moon and stars have been our constant companions as they repeat their paths and patterns across the skies. We continue to turn to the cosmos for guidance, trusting in the deep and abiding wisdom of the universe as we strive for fulfilment, truth and understanding.

The most basic and familiar aspect of astrology draws on the twelve signs of the zodiac, each connected to a unique constellation as well as its own particular colours, numbers and characteristics. These twelve familiar signs are also known as the sun signs: Aries, Taurus, Gemini, Cancer, Leo, Virgo, Libra, Scorpio, Sagittarius, Capricorn, Aquarius and Pisces.

Aries   Taurus   Gemini   Cancer   Leo   Virgo

Libra   Scorpio   Sagittarius   Capricorn   Aquarius   Pisces

Each sign is associated with an element (fire, air, earth or water), and also carries a particular quality: cardinal (action-takers), fixed (steady and constant) and mutable (changeable and transformational). Beginning to understand these complex combinations, and to recognize the layered influences they bring to bear on your life, will unlock your own potential for personal insight, self-awareness and discovery.

In our data-flooded lives, now more than ever it can be difficult to know where to turn for guidance and advice. With your astrology oracle always by your side, navigating life's twists and turns will become a smoother, more mindful process. Harness the prescience of the stars and tune in to the resonance of your sun sign with this wisdom-packed guide that will lead you to greater self-knowledge and deeper confidence in the decisions you are making. Of course, not all questions are created equal; your unique character, your circumstances and the issues with which you find yourself confronted all add up to a conundrum unlike any other... but with your question in mind and your zodiac oracle in your hand, you're already halfway to the answer.

Aquarius
JANUARY 20 TO FEBRUARY 18

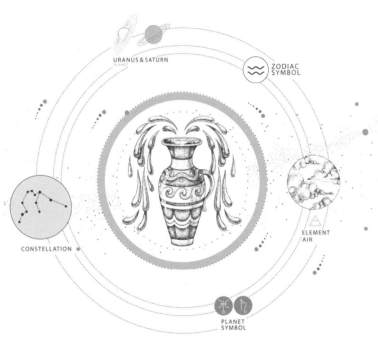

Element: Air

Quality: Fixed

Named for the constellation: Aquarius (the water-bearer)

Ruled by: Uranus and Saturn

Opposite: Leo

Characterized by: Optimism, independence, positivity

Colours: Silver, blue

How to Use This Book

You can engage with your oracle whenever you need to but, for best results, create an atmosphere of calm and quiet, somewhere you will not be disturbed, making a place for yourself and your question to take priority. Whether this is a particular physical area you turn to in times of contemplation, or whether you need to fence off a dedicated space within yourself during your busy day, that all depends on you and your circumstances. Whichever you choose, it is essential that you actively put other thoughts and distractions to one side in order to concentrate upon the question you wish to answer.

Find a comfortable position, cradle this book lightly in your hands, close your eyes, centre yourself. Focus on the question you wish to ask. Set your intention gently and mindfully towards your desire to answer this question, to the exclusion of all other thoughts and mind-chatter. Allow all else to float softly away, as you remain quiet and still, gently watching the shape and form of the question you wish to address. Gently deepen and slow your breathing.

Tune in to the ancient resonance of your star sign, the vibrations of your surroundings, the beat of your heart and the flow of life and the universe moving in and around you. You are one with the universe.

Now simply press the book between your palms as you clearly and distinctly ask your question (whether aloud or in your head), then open it at any page. Open your eyes. Your advice will be revealed.

Read it carefully. Take your time turning this wisdom over in your mind, allowing your thoughts to surround it, to absorb it, flow with it, then to linger and settle where they will.

Remember, your oracle will not provide anything as blunt and brutal as a completely literal answer. That is not its role. Rather, you will be gently guided towards the truth you seek through your own consciousness, experience and understanding. And as a result, you will grow, learn and flourish.

Let's begin.

Close your eyes.

Hold the question you want
answered clearly in your mind.

Open your oracle to any page to
reveal your cosmic insight.

Spend some time inside
your own head Aquarius – you will
find the answer there.

Time to stop just dreaming
about a change of direction; take
some positive steps to make
it happen.

You often prefer turning inwards
on yourself Aquarius, but be sure not
to travel so deep that you get lost in
your own thoughts.

If you are noticing things
about yourself that need improvement,
don't turn a blind eye. Setbacks
are as important to the process
as successes.

The water-bearer, ruled by
the air, you are a complicated creature
Aquarius, and difficult to categorize.
Everyone knows that you're an
original, which, of course, is
just as you like it.

Stay focused on the future
and all will be well.

Give others the gift of your
energy and focus Aquarius – they may
be vying for your attention and right
now you may well be in a position
to give it to them.

Self-discipline will be essential
in crafting those major changes you
have dreamed of Aquarius; there is no
time like the present to start taking the
practical steps necessary to make your
dreams come true.

Don't be sidetracked by
questions and circular arguments
Aquarius. You will not achieve
the focus you need to get this done
if you allow your imagination to
run away with you.

Visualizing change is only the
first step. Time to put that Aquarian
imagination to good use:
make a plan.

If you are finding your
energy drained by the demands
and expectations of others, now is
the time to take a break, to rest and
recharge. You cannot drink from an
empty cup, and you cannot serve
others from an empty
vessel either.

Put your belief in the power
of positive change to good use.
Make it happen.

You're a visionary creative Aquarius, and your determination to frame this issue in the most visually pleasing way will ensure a good result.

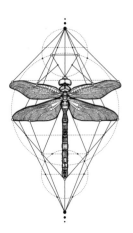

You will need to switch on those legendary problem-solving skills for this one. Your answer lies within the question.

A strong compromise is a better resolution than a unilateral win. You will need to work past your cherished ideals on this one.

It is very tempting to ask only
the safe questions, especially when
you are sure of the answer. Now ask
the real question.

No one can fault your big-picture approach, but perhaps this one might benefit from extra time spent sifting through the finer details. A little more focus is needed.

Not every sign is as good at problem-solving as you Aquarius, and that's why they so often get it wrong. Time to bring some of your visionary vitality into play, to help others see the best way forwards.

Remind yourself of your
original goal and check that you
haven't accidentally veered off course.
Interruptions are never far from your
door Aquarius, but perseverance and
dedicated effort will get you there.
Stay on track.

Might you be focusing a bit too hard on the outcome you think you want? It's worth considering. Don't let an opportunity pass you by.

Your original approach will be
the key to success but remember to
let others add their thoughts –
everyone likes to be heard.

Take some time to recharge;
frustration and overload will cloud
your thinking.

Work through only the most
immediate problem Aquarius,
then modify your expectations and
adopt a more flexible approach
as you move on.

You are a pure Aquarian idealist,
every step of the way – nothing less
than perfect will do. It pays off usually,
but some things just look better a little
less polished.

Yes, it goes against all your better Aquarian instincts to agree without some thorough research, and yes, you're right, you do usually know best. But this time, try simply saying 'Yes'. Something unexpected might happen.

Of course you're not cold,
and you're certainly not uncaring, it's
just that sometimes you have bigger
things on your mind. Try tuning in to
what's going on with those around
you right now – staying too far inside
your own head might prevent you
reaching your full potential.

The decision to do what is right is not always the easiest path to follow. But it is your path.

Your stars have gifted you with remarkable powers of intelligence and a strong sense of justice – but don't cloud the matter by focusing on your preferred outcome. Allow any, then see what comes.

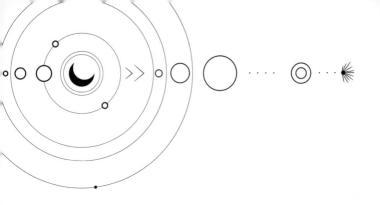

Investigate further, as a matter of urgency Aquarius. The details may differ from those you noted at first, cursory glance.

You are fully entitled to the love
you need; do not hesitate to speak up
and claim what you deserve. If it is not
available from this source, move on.

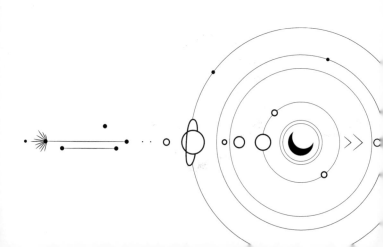

Firm conclusions and workable solutions don't always result, no matter how much time we sink into thinking things through. If insights escape you, just move on. Most likely the answers will finally pop up and surprise you once you are already engrossed in something else.

Given to living so much in
your own head, you can sometimes
forget to take proper care of yourself
Aquarius. Be assured: some proper
nourishment will help you turn
everything around, and you will feel
much more in control.

Aquarian uniqueness is second to none, that goes without saying. But is it always necessary to start from the ground up with the original thinking? Sometimes, standing on the shoulders of giants is a perfectly acceptable way to reach those higher goals, and it gets you there just that little bit quicker.

No need to make a sacrifice
to achieve this one; the universe
is primed to reward you
regardless. Enjoy!

Inside your head is your haven, and of course that makes perfect sense given how interesting it is in there. But try popping out every now and then, for some fresh air and to dust yourself off a little. This is an ideal time to try to be a little more present.

Resist the urge to focus on
too big a picture this time; all this
'formulating the best plan in the world'
is admirable, but getting it done is
what actually matters.

Intention or action?
It's time to make your decision.

Of course, you are a uniquely innovative thinker with lots of essential outcomes entirely dependent on your intellectual rigour. But now might be one of those rare and delicious times you should just relax and treat yourself to what you fancy. And maybe another one after that.

Take the time to climb a hill,
fly a kite or just stare off into the
mid-distance today; you need the
air around you to gain some
perspective on this one.

Soaringly idealistic and free-thinking, reaching for the stars is home from home for you (you are an air sign, after all). But try staying grounded for this one – you have so much potential down here on Earth, and you just might surprise yourself.

Show yourself some love
Aquarius, and give that hard-working
brain of yours a blast of fresh air
for five minutes. Stargazing,
cloud-spotting, birdwatching, maybe
even an outdoor headstand... just allow
yourself to be for a while.

Anything is possible, as you well know. Try approaching this one from a different angle or looking at it through a different lens.

With personal goals now within
your reach, there is a real glow
around you Aquarius. If entering into
negotiations, ensure you do so with
full confidence; you can do this.

When collaboration is required, your free-spirited approach can really come into its own and show everyone the way to do things in a fresher, less conventional, more effective way. Let your light shine Aquarius.

You are so self-sufficient
and independent Aquarius, that
it's sometimes hard to imagine there
might be anything you can't do all by
yourself. But try to accept help this
time – it might make things that
little bit easier.

Relinquishing control can feel risky...
But on this occasion a detail-oriented
angle is the only way to achieve a fair
and balanced outcome. Others have
more patience for the detail than
you do. Go with it.

Listen, focus, notice, feel, acknowledge, stay present.

Forgive others and yourself for
mistakes made on life's path.

Remember that taking care
of yourself means nourishing soul,
mind and body. If you can find a way
to combine the three, you'll be
satisfying your heart's desire
for ideal outcomes as well!

With Leo as your opposite sign, sometimes you need to take a break from your thinking mind and trust your intuition to spark a few flames for you. Now is one of those times.

There is a bright future ahead
for this venture, despite difficulties you
might be experiencing at present.
Maintain a long-term, pragmatic
approach Aquarius.

Finding it difficult to get a grip at the moment Aquarius? You might not be the only one – it's a frustrating time, with everything blowing all over the place. Don't take your frustrations out on others, and don't let them take their frustrations out on you.

Being true to yourself can take
a lot of courage Aquarius, especially if
you are usually a conflict-avoider. Be
braver than usual now; you are acting
for the right reasons.

If your intuition raises an alert
that you are suddenly in the wrong
place, or the wrong company, take
quick and decisive steps to correct
your situation Aquarius.
Listen to yourself.

Hold fast to your own beliefs Aquarius, and be sure that your decisions are on the course plotted using your trusty moral compass.

The success of those
close to you also serves to raise you
up. Celebrate their wins with a
generous, loving spirit.

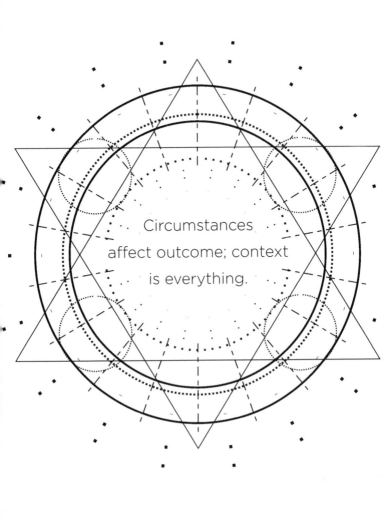

Circumstances affect outcome; context is everything.

The universe will ensure
that you are rarely short of amusing,
challenging and diverting company,
should you desire it. Remember, a true
friend is one who tells you what
you need to hear rather than
what you want to hear.

When you are in the spotlight,
make good use of the focus Aquarius.
With plenty of attention coming your
way, you have an opportunity
to make a big splash.

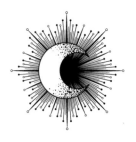

It's important that the give and
take in your work and personal
relationships makes sense to you
Aquarius, otherwise it is easy to lose
momentum and the desire to carry on.
Time for a bit of an audit. If anything
seems off-centre, now is the time
to adjust your settings.

Overcoming obstacles is a
particular skill of yours Aquarius,
whether you negotiate them or simply
ignore them until they dissolve into
thin air. That talent will serve
you well now.

Self-doubt won't do you any good;
resist second guessing on this one.

The circumstances might not
be quite as they seem – take another
look before you make your decision.

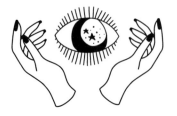

Have a break from tending
to the low hum of constant thinking
generated by your busy brain and
instead digest the opinions of a
trusted adviser or two. This one is best
not tackled alone and your internal
monologue might not be giving
you the clearest steer.

Try as you might, even you
cannot rewrite the past. But your
future is entirely in your
own hands.

Resist the urge to pick
a path while your emotions
are in charge.

Yes, you can.

But that doesn't mean you should.

Own up to what
you don't know Aquarius, and
ask for any help you need.

When you are finding things
a struggle, it can be difficult to make
sure that everyone else is having fun.
Don't concern yourself with others
right now, it's time to give something
back to yourself and prioritize your
own contentment first.

The big things take up more head space, inevitably. But don't forget to pay attention to the smaller details that pave the way, or at least task someone you can trust with keeping them in order.

You don't need to justify yourself
– it is obvious what you are capable
of, and if others can't appreciate
that, well that is their problem.
Go with the flow.

Pick a path and stride
out confidently. Life is too short
for dithering at the crossroads.

The answer is something
deeper and less tangible than the
easy fix you are considering.

Change is coming Aquarius,
and you may well need to bow your
head and lean into the wind if you
are to weather this storm. Hang in
there, it will pass.

It is never too late for an
apology, and if you are giving one
then be sure to make it count.

Turn your attention inwards
Aquarius – there is a wellbeing
to-do list as long as your arm pinned
up in there and it's time you gave
it some attention. Time for a
self-focused spring clean.

The answer is right
in front of you; do the thing
you won't regret later on.

Clearheaded and idealistic, you
are also a determined individual, in
true Aquarius style. But your logical
approach might mean you miss out
on an opportunity now and
then. Take a chance.

You are brave and clever
Aquarius; persevere and you
will get there.

When you know what it is you
really want, there is nothing more
powerful than that big-picture view
Aquarians are so famous for.

As a water-carrying air sign,
high pressure can feel overwhelming
to you. Take shelter for a little while,
until life starts to show signs of
beginning to settle again.

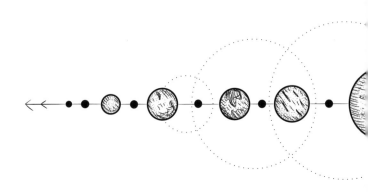

Take your time to process
changes and understand their
implications. Trust in the planets'
ability to support you during this time.
Keep everything flowing through.

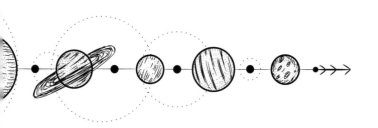

Quiet time for reflection and
meditation will help to support your
sleep and nurture your soul.

Your typically great Aquarian
memory might be a particular asset
at the moment, but you will need to
relax enough to let the wisdom it
holds rise to the surface.

When you feel your sparkle is
shining a little less brightly than
normal, take it as a sign that you
need to make some time for yourself
– time for warmth, cosy textures
and feeding your body and soul.
Nourish, nurture, replenish.

Stay close to home, literally and metaphorically. Hold those you cherish close and acknowledge what your heart needs.

When temptation strikes, your
self-discipline will be tested. Draw
on that energy that your ruling planet
Uranus brings and your willpower will
prove stronger than ever.

Relinquish this problem to the universe and accept the powerful energy it sends you in return. You have plenty of backbone and willingness to stay on the right path.

Do not be tempted away from what you know is right by pretty trinkets or false promises. Reinforce your own beliefs and remind yourself of your personal goals and values. Remain steadfast.

Your aim is true with this one
Aquarius, and your suspicions and
ideas are right on target. Don't let
others put you off; you know
what you know.

If an opportunity you thought you'd missed appears again, be ready to grasp it with both hands. It doesn't need to be the one that got away any longer.

Do not hesitate to make the most of an exciting possibility Aquarius. Your unconventional free-spiritedness will be a distinct asset in securing the thing you desire, and it will also push you on towards more exciting changes in the future.

With your clear-headed
Aquarian independence, your
intellectual ability and the love and
support of friends and/or family, there
is nothing you cannot achieve right
now. Throw your energies into
exploring all possibilities.

Sometimes the universe
decides it's time for you to make
a big decision, whether you feel ready
or not. Draw a lesson from your
opposite sign, the lion-hearted Leo,
and make a bold, brave choice rather
than a wobbly, uncertain one.

Perhaps you feel trapped,
tied down in a testing situation
Aquarius, one from which you long
to free yourself. If so, now is your
moment to slip like a cloud from
those bonds that seem to hold you.
Once released, move forwards
without looking back.

If you are feeling unhappy
or unfulfilled, now is the time to look
deep within and ask yourself what it is
you really want. Be honest with
yourself and engage that analytical
part of your Aquarius skill-set to help
you. For such a forward-oriented sign,
it is vital that you can shape your
future into an appealing destination.

It looks like you have some tough decisions to make at the moment Aquarius – best to tackle these now to avoid regrets at a later stage.

Daydreaming isn't always a case of flitting around inside your own fanciful thoughts, in fact far from it Aquarius. The images and ideas you are imagining have a crucial role to play in shaping your next steps and fashioning your approach.

Persist with expressing the
ideas you feel you need to share, even
if they are not as well received at first
as you might like. It's important that
you air what's on your mind.

Your idealistic Aquarian nature
can lead you to dissatisfaction,
even jealousy, when it seems that
things aren't stacking up the way you
would like. Resist the temptation to
compare your situation with that of
others; remember that what is right for
them (and the price they are willing
to pay) might not suit you so well.

When it comes to your friendships,
you believe in freedom and openness.
Envy and jealousy are poisonous. Be
open and honest with yourself and
acknowledge that you have
some work to do.

Commitment to justice and positive change are your strongest guiding principles Aquarius. Remember to engage your problem-solving brain to find the best ways of communicating these to others – not everyone speaks the same language.

Don't allow the sheer volume
of your own thoughts to distract you
right now Aquarius – others are
waiting for your move.

It's important to make time to spend with the people you love Aquarius, even if finding a time that suits everyone can be more difficult than you expect. Be patient but persist.

Negotiation doesn't come
naturally to everyone, especially
when compromise is also involved.
Teach by example Aquarius, and ease
the frustration others might be
feeling by paying attention.

Time to be bold Aquarius;
there is no room for subtlety with
this one unfortunately. It's essential
that you make yourself seen
and heard.

Famously original and inventive (some might even say eccentric), you Aquarians have the most innovative problem-solving skills of all the signs. Use them wisely right now and don't be swayed off-course by other trifling matters that might be clamouring for your attention.

Things are not always one way
or the other with you Aquarius, and
feeling torn between wanting
company and wanting to be alone is
not an uncommon dilemma. Choose
company if you can bear it, but be
selective and keep it short.

It is important now to listen to your heart rather than your head Aquarius – the two are likely pulling you in opposite directions. But be assured, the heart knows. Let it speak up.

There are no hidden surprises
with this one; if you feel that you
already know what it's all about,
you're probably right.

Spend some time putting
your vision into action Aquarius,
then use your air-sign powered
gift of communication to tell
everyone about it.

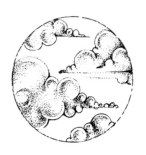

A collaborative environment is nectar to your bee Aquarius, but that doesn't mean that your ideas are always best executed in a group. Take some time to straighten things out and hone your thoughts before you share them – ironing out the wrinkles before wearing this one in public is advisable.

People-pleasing can be a particular problem for you Aquarius, leaving you drained and a bit cold – it's such a lot of effort after all. Take a step back for a couple of days and see what happens. Let them come to you

Possessiveness is not usually
in your nature Aquarius, so it can
surprise you as much as everyone else
when it rears its head. Sharing is much
more your style, but if that's not how
you're feeling right now, then so
be it. Listen to yourself.

Visionary Aquarians can find
it tremendously difficult, almost
impossible, to embrace contentment
in their own lives... it seems there is
always something else to strive for,
some crucial component just out of
reach. Adopt a pragmatic approach
this time and advise yourself as you
would advise someone else
you really care about.

Your daily routine often follows
a predictable rhythm as the hours
blend into days, blend into weeks...
Remind yourself that this is all basic
groundwork – excitement is out there
for you to grab if you want it, but
first you need to have this base
structure firmly in place.

Time for some soul-food and
self-love Aquarius; it's all too easy
to get stuck in a pattern of not giving
back to yourself. Lavish yourself with
some nourishment and attention.

With so much going on and
so many people demanding your
attention, you run the risk of feeling
overwhelmed. But take a deep breath,
soak it up and enjoy it Aquarius – it all
comes from a place of pure love.

Reflecting the positivity of others is more important than ever right now Aquarius. Keep the emotional vibrations high and your space will resonate with all the love, light and energy you are creating.

Maintain free-flowing communication, open the conduits to give and receive, and allow energy to keep moving. Don't try to fix anyone else to an opinion or a decision, or to confirm an outcome Aquarius. That is not the right way to work through this one.

Keep everything light right now Aquarius; there is nothing to be gained by going against your nature and looking for nailed-down decisions and fixed finish points. There is always something that comes after and something that came before.

If something or someone from
the past suddenly reappears or
memories are crowding your head,
there's a good chance there's a
message for you in there somewhere.
Think carefully about what's going on
right now, and whether lessons
from your past could help.

Heart and head often pull
you in different directions Aquarius,
but each has an important role to play
in guiding you to the right place. Right
now, although it's endlessly tricky,
try to accommodate both.

Difficult decisions might leave
you confused right now Aquarius;
it can feel as though there is no right
answer. Don't let the seemingly
impossible drain your energy; don't
make those commitments or decisions
until the point you absolutely have to,
and then just do what feels right.

Super-serious is really not your style Aquarius, but it is where you've been staying recently. Raise your vibrations with some connecting and some conversing – bounce a bit of energy around and feel the difference it makes.

The past is a treasure trove of valuable lessons; forget them at your peril. Aiming for a different result but making all the same mistakes is never going to work.

Keeping things upbeat will
make for more effective and
productive conversations Aquarius –
suddenly much more will seem
possible. Keep the ideas flowing and
the energy-exchange moving.

No one could deny that you're
a thinker Aquarius, and with intuition
and originality high on your traits list
there is a lot you can bring to solving
this one. With the right audience
(remember, this won't be for everyone)
your suggestions will receive
a warm welcome.

Your intuition is not leading
you astray right now Aquarius.
Others might assume you are being
hasty, over-sensitive or perhaps
unnecessarily dramatic, but pay no
attention to them. You are
completely on target.

If you find your focus slipping
a bit today Aquarius, don't be
disheartened. Embrace this
opportunity to see things
from different angles.

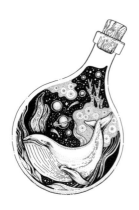

Achieving resolutions and outcomes might be overrated Aquarius; after all, isn't everything in a constant state of flux, with all the uncertainty and continual movement that entails?

This might be the time for exploring options rather than nailing down solutions Aquarius.

Gathering information and researching facts is a good use of your time right now. You are not in any position to consider making a decision until you have a handle on the details.

It may be difficult to take control today Aquarius. Sometimes trying to manage all aspects feels like trying to bail out a leaky boat with a teaspoon... while it's raining. Consider whether you might be approaching this problem in the wrong way, or flip that over and ask yourself whether there might be a better way to do this.

Keep it light Aquarius, and make
sure you keep everything moving
cleanly and continually through.
Thrown open the windows, breathe
it in and let the breeze blow
the cobwebs away.

Sometimes those who
mean well have a funny way of
showing it; the desire to be involved
(read: interfere) can be stronger than
the desire to do the right thing. Helpful
comments might seem harsh and
'constructive criticism' might really
grind you down. Keep your barrier
raised Aquarius and shelter
safely behind it.

Reinforcing your undertaking
to approach this in a positive frame
of mind might seem more arduous and
less simple than it sounds Aquarius.
Absorb feedback consciously, process
it constructively and use it
to your advantage.

Criticism can sting Aquarius,
but finding a way to deflect the hurt
while at the same time absorbing the
information will set you on a stronger
and more self-sufficient path. There is
learning to be gained in all situations.
Consider it all, then discard anything
you have no use for.

Sometimes things seem
easy and sometimes they are
a lot more difficult. You can't let
up at the moment Aquarius, which
might feel frustrating as you've been
working so hard. But you need to
persist if you are to achieve that
attention and acknowledgement
you are aiming for.

Powering constantly ahead at full pace might be starting to take a toll Aquarius. Take a strategic look at all your responsibilities and think carefully about whether there might be a way to share the load more evenly.

Pay close attention to your inner voice Aquarius. If an upcoming event is stoking your anxiety, it might be that you haven't yet made the correct decision about your next steps.

Taking a break from all the pressures will not really be possible until you, well, take a break from all the pressures Aquarius. Time to be a grown-up about this and schedule the time you need in the place you need it. It's for your own good.

Recharging is not going to be as simple as a weekend away or sleeping in for a few days. You need a deeper overhaul Aquarius, more of a long-term approach than a quick repair job. It will take time.

Carefully pinpoint the desire
that lies behind this impulse, then
interrogate it. Does it arise from a
place of wholeness and love, or is it
driven by a hunger or particular
emptiness? Address the root of the
problem, rather than the symptoms.

Allow your ambition to take
the lead Aquarius; it is time to follow
your dreams to a bigger, brighter
future. Others will notice the change in
you and perhaps feel compelled to
support or even join you.

As an air sign Aquarius,
you must make sure you have enough
mental stimulation to keep your
brain busy. Otherwise your
motivation will weaken.

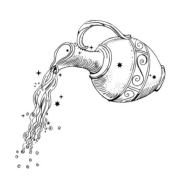

Feeling constrained is not
for you Aquarius; you need freedom to
move, to find your own way.

Differing views might cause
a clash; stay out of the way until the
storm-threat dies down.

You might not be the biggest fan of what's been going on, but that doesn't mean you need to add your voice to the wave of criticism Aquarius.

Material possessions are not
the answer to spiritual emptiness.
Seek out the real problem Aquarius,
then address that.

Deeper and less tangible issues
must first be recognized and
dealt with Aquarius.

Your loved ones depend on your
support and understanding Aquarius,
even though you might not always
realize it. Sharing time together
is all that is required of you.

Intuition can be both a blessing
and a curse, but it is integral to the
way you live your life. Sometimes,
however, it can be overly distracting
and may even threaten to pull your
attention unhelpfully sideways.
For the moment, focus on the
practical if you can.

If the involvement of difficult personalities is making things tricky, try turning this over to look for the benefits they bring.

Stay as neutral as you can
right now Aquarius; views might differ,
but all are valid and should be
treated as such.

You will not effortlessly connect
with everyone Aquarius. But others
have their own challenges and letting
them get under your skin is
counterproductive.

The present is everything
Aquarius, but the past holds
many lessons and the future much
possibility. All is connected. All flows
forwards and backwards.

Difficulties are not yours to face alone Aquarius – those you love stand strong alongside you. When you need them, they will be right there for you.

Not knowing is not a problem
– you just have to find the right person
to ask. Not knowing and not asking
because of pride is a problem.
Don't let it be yours.

You are quick to adapt to
different energies around you
Aquarius, but you also need plenty of
alone time to refresh yourself. Follow
your intuition when this desire
is upon you.

Learning to trust others can
be tremendously difficult for you
Aquarius. Perhaps this issue presents
an opportunity to practice expressing
yourself in a new and different way.

Guard against destructive or negative external energies Aquarius – if you can remove yourself from their influence, so much the better.

Speak up for yourself and
voice your own opinions. Waiting for
someone to ask what you think is not
a risk worth taking.

You don't have to answer everybody's questions, but overt secrecy will inevitably allow suspicion to take hold. Reassure others of your intentions as far as you are comfortable.

It is a beautiful gift of your
sign that you see the world as full of
possibilities. Embrace that attitude
and spread the positivity. There are
some who will greatly benefit
from hearing your message.

Preparing for the future should not obscure the importance of living your life today Aquarius. But do consider the long-term benefits of a little groundwork here and there.

If others seek your advice,
take the responsibility seriously
Aquarius. Do not get swept up in the
thrill of others' good opinions of you,
but rather be sure that you are
answering them with due
care and consideration.

Trust your own instincts Aquarius;
the wisdom you are seeking already
lies deep within yourself.

Others trying to get too
close too soon might lead you to
adopt your fallback chilly defensive
posture. Explain your reasons,
if you feel it is necessary.

Unfinished issues may linger and cause confusion, especially if you have done all you think is required to shut them down now. Allow your intuition to guide you to the solution.

The frustrations of today may simply melt away over the next little while Aquarius – don't waste too much time or energy wrestling with them yet.

Untangling some knotty issues
will allow you to proceed smoothly
into the next phase. Don't store up
tasks like this for tomorrow, if
you can sweep them out of
the way now.

You have more freedom than
perhaps you had realized Aquarius;
don't take this for granted.

Sometimes pleasure has a price
Aquarius. Check yourself before you
invest too much in something that is
not likely to deliver.

The fix you seek can't be
delivered by courier, or posted
through the letterbox, or carted home
in a (tastefully designed) giftbag.
Take comfort and guidance from your
close advisors Aquarius – they will
show you the way.

Retain your focus and take full advantage of any professional opportunities that come your way right now Aquarius.

Don't forget to attend to your personal life; it might be difficult trying to juggle this along with everything else, but your needs and the needs of those you love must take priority.

Success comes in many
different guises Aquarius, and
who's to say you can't have them all?
Ride the wave that's coming your way
and keep your eyes open.

Your idiosyncratic approach
can sometimes leave others a little
perplexed Aquarius, but doing things
your way is just so you. It will all make
sense to them once you have moved
things on a little more.

Inspire others to come along
with you on the solving-rather-than-
complaining train Aquarius. Ultimately,
you'll all enjoy it a lot more.

You're famously independent Aquarius, but if the to-do list is piling up it might be time to call in some assistance. It need only be a pragmatic temporary solution – you can handle it.

If you are not comfortable with a particular request, simply refuse. It is not even necessary to give a reason (although if you can it might help things go a little more smoothly).

Try to see an issue arising at the moment as an opportunity rather than an obstacle. If you approach this with the right frame of mind, everyone stands to benefit.

Patience and persistence
will be the keys to success
Aquarius. Don't allow sticky
details to lure you into
circling back.

You will require willpower and
strength of purpose Aquarius, but you
already know the right decision to
make. It's all just a matter of
timing now.

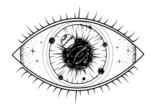

Holding your own doesn't
mean you need to approach
every interaction like a battle
Aquarius. Sometimes it is as well to
observe and wait to find out
what's required of you.

Embrace opportunities for
partnership and connection right now
Aquarius; there is no better feeling
than when the energy flows in .
both directions.

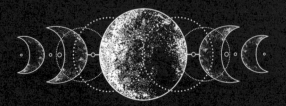

Avoid being dragged into
other people's dramas Aquarius;
your involvement at this time will
not benefit anyone.

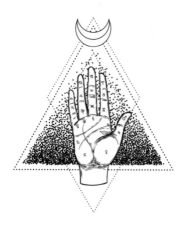

Time to make a call Aquarius.
Even if you don't feel fully ready, you
will need to choose a direction and
make a move soon.

With Leo as your opposite sign,
sometimes you need to remember
that a louder roar may occasionally
yield more immediate results. Try it.

The feelings of others are
very much not under your control –
consider all the unrelated factors that
feed into any individual's experience.
Release yourself from that sense
of responsibility.

Taking the long view will serve
you better right now Aquarius, there
is no need to bother yourself with
details at this point.

A tidal change is on its way.
Stay open to the new possibilities it
will bring, rather than just drifting
along with the strongest current.

Embrace opportunities to
achieve a more harmonious balance;
all is positive and your responses
should reflect that.

Your confidence will benefit
enormously from a particular refusal
you need to make right now, despite
some pretty strong emotional
persuasion. Steel yourself
and get it done.

Consider presenting ideas for solutions rather than just calling out the problems Aquarius. It's a distinction worth making, and one that increases your chances of a positive reception.

It's not always essential to understand every single detail before you join in a new venture, but it is a good idea to at least know that you will all be pulling in the same direction.

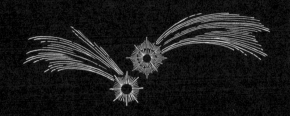

Your current concern requires
a splash of spontaneity Aquarius. Time
to take a leap of faith.

Your gut instinct will lead you
to the solution and tell you plenty
more along the way if you're in the
mood for listening. Feeling, rather
than thinking, is required.

The unconventional is to be expected of you Aquarius; you are ruled by Uranus after all. But with disruption and change at the heart of your planet's traits, your determination to do things your own way is about to really pay off.

Eccentric or original? It probably depends who you ask. But one thing is for sure – you tend to spend very little time considering what others think of you. There's no reason this time should be any different.

It is vital that you keep
everything flowing; drawing in oxygen
is easier when you keep moving
Aquarius.

Of course the more complicated questions often yield the most interesting answers Aquarius, but you need to take this one back to basics before you can really get stuck into interrogating it. Work through the simple stuff first.

Other people so often seem
wrapped up in petty concerns,
not worthy of your time and attention.
Don't allow yourself to become
distracted; you have much more
important issues to attend to.

Ultimately, you are one of the loners of the zodiac Aquarius. If compromise feels like giving too much away, be honest with others about where you see this going (or not going). Don't waste anyone's time. Especially not your own.

Over-thinking this one
won't pay off Aquarius; how
you see it is how it is.

Your skill at adapting your energy to suit the situation is second to none. But don't exhaust yourself with all that shape-shifting or hide too much of your true self.

Try not to obsess about what others might be thinking; you must do what you think is right. They will inevitably draw their own conclusions.

Really, right now the
decision you need to make is all
about whether to hold on or to let go.
Letting go will mean releasing into
trust. Holding on will be a
struggle if this is not
meant to be.

Bide your time and reserve your energy for now Aquarius. Keep your powder dry until you really need it.

Trying to be in two places at once just won't work Aquarius. But hold those you love in your thoughts and be sure you show up for them when they really need you.

Unencumbered and unfettered
as the breeze is your favourite state of
being Aquarius. Make the most of your
freedom: catch the wind and soar
upwards while you can.

Keep your eyes open and your mind sharp. With so much going on right now, you need to know what's happening around you.

Don't be tempted to over-think things right now Aquarius – take it all at face value and see what transpires. Everything might be exactly as it seems.

Don't be tempted by the
lure of dreams and fanciful
impossibilities when what you have,
right now, is real and tangible and,
let's be honest, pretty good.

Uncertain times call for
decisive actions Aquarius. Gather
as much information as you can, by all
means. But when it comes down to it,
your decision must be based on what
your instinct is telling you.

Try to see all the different
sides of this issue Aquarius; if you can
flow around it to understand its true
shape, you will have a much better
idea of how to deal with it.

You love bringing fresh and unique ideas to the table, like the true water-bearer you are. Apply this skill to any work or personal relationships that are at the forefront for you right now Aquarius.

Keep your energy flowing
and the ideas will continue Aquarius.
Communication and creativity are your
magical powers right now, and it feels
like anything is possible.

The admiration of others can
be very flattering. Receive any
compliments graciously and share
something in return if you are
able to do so honestly.

Trying to grind down the
details or attempting to over-analyse
the situation will get you nowhere
Aquarius. Insights are great,
but don't force too close a focus.

Don't allow yourself to be lured into
a trap or blindsided by the unexpected
today Aquarius; keep your eyes and
ears open, and stay alert.

If it feels that those around you are more sensitive or perhaps touchier than usual, keep to yourself a little more than you ordinarily would, to reduce unnecessary friction.

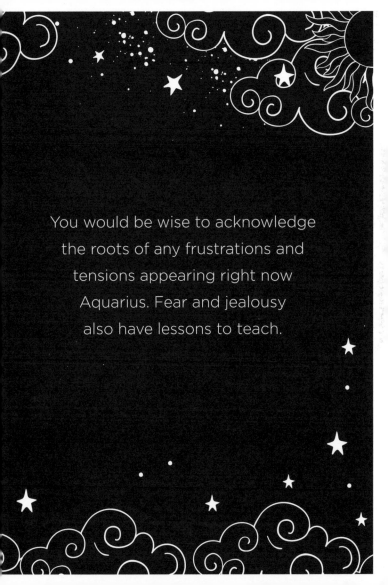

You would be wise to acknowledge
the roots of any frustrations and
tensions appearing right now
Aquarius. Fear and jealousy
also have lessons to teach.

Avoid making any agreements
or commitments right now, strong
as the urge to finalize things might
be. It would be sensible to wait a little
longer, so you can be sure of
what will be required.

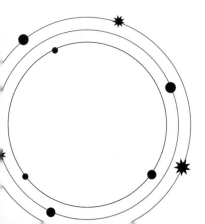

Imagination and intuition will guide you as reliably as facts and figures on this one Aquarius. You are still at the stage where anything is possible.

Your desire for meaning and truth may shortly manifest in the opportunity for an exciting, fresh adventure Aquarius.

Your supreme adaptability and resilience mean that you are better equipped than most to cope with change Aquarius. But really, it's very simple – you like change. Help others learn to see it your way.

If you can't shake the feeling
that something is missing, or has been
forgotten, allow yourself time to pause
before moving on. Given a little
breathing space, your reminder will
very likely bob up to the surface.

Establishing a routine may be important for you right now Aquarius... adhering to a schedule will allow you more planned and predictable breaks. If your energy drops too low, it will take additional effort to haul everything back on track.

Taking time to reflect will remind you to put yourself first more often Aquarius. Soften your approach to yourself a little and spend some time nurturing the child within.

Rushing on ahead will only mean
more to do later when it comes to
reviewing and fixing. Make it easy on
yourself in the long-term, and
finish what you start.

Reconnecting with emotions you have been denying or avoiding recently is tremendously important Aquarius. If you fail to deal with these issues now, there will be a lot of messy backtracking to do later.

Ideas and intuition are much more
likely to bubble up to the surface if
you allow yourself that essential time
to rest and rejuvenate. Balance is all.

Forcing your mind to grapple with a particular issue right now is the fastest route to nowhere. Make a conscious decision to leave this to one side for now. In the meantime, the answer might materialize when you least expect it.

Following your intuition
might lead to a significant change in
direction Aquarius. Time for some
clean finishes and some
fresh new starts.

Broadening your horizons
will consolidate your own
understanding and learning
Aquarius. Spread your wings.

New experiences will be enriching
Aquarius; embrace them.

An option that might seem confusing or outside of your comfort zone right now will bring rewards and spark your creativity further down the line Aquarius. Be bold.